Technology in **MOTION**

How to Build
CARS

Rita Storey

 Crabtree Publishing Company
www.crabtreebooks.com

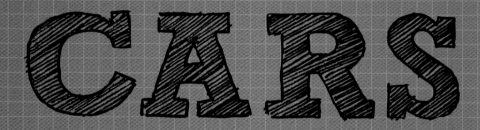

Technology in MOTION

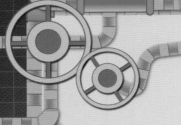

Crabtree Publishing Company
www.crabtreebooks.com
1-800-387-7650

Published in Canada
Crabtree Publishing
616 Welland Avenue
St. Catharines, ON
L2M 5V6

Published in the United States
Crabtree Publishing
PMB 59051
350 Fifth Ave, 59th Floor
New York, NY 10118

Published in 2017 by CRABTREE PUBLISHING COMPANY.

First published in 2016 by The Watts Publishing Group (A division of Hachette Children's Books)
Copyright © The Watts Publishing Group 2016

Author: Rita Storey

Editorial director: Adrian Cole

Project coordinator: Kathy Middleton

Editors: Petrice Custance

Designer manager: Peter Scoulding

Cover design and illustrations: Cathryn Gilbert

Proofreader: Wendy Scavuzzo

Prepress technician: Samara Parent

Print and production coordinator: Katherine Berti

The publisher would like to thank the following for their kind permission to reproduce their photographs:

Land Rover MENA; Rob Bulmahn 17; Flock and Siemens 9; Wikimedia Commons: 4, 5.

Step-by-step photography by Tudor Photography, Banbury.

Printed in Hong Kong/012017/BK20171024

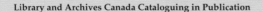

Library and Archives Canada Cataloguing in Publication

Derrington, Louise, author
Storey, Rita, author
        How to build cars / Rita Storey.

(Technology in motion)
Issued in print and electronic formats.
ISBN 978-0-7787-3393-5 (hardback).--
ISBN 978-0-7787-3396-6 (paperback).--
ISBN 978-1-4271-1907-0 (html)

        1. Automobiles--Design and construction--Juvenile literature. 2. Automobiles--Models--Design and construction--Juvenile literature. I. Title.

TL240.S865 2016   j629.222   C2016-906629-0
                                                          C2016-906630-4

Library of Congress Cataloging-in-Publication Data

Names: Storey, Rita, author.
Title: How to build cars / Rita Storey.
Description: New York, NY : Crabtree Publishing Company, 2017.
    Series: Technology in motion | "First published in 2016 by
    The Watts Publishing Group." | Audience: Ages 10-14. |
    Audience: Grades 7 to 8. | Includes index.
Identifiers: LCCN 2016045810 (print) | LCCN 2016048348 (ebook)
    ISBN 9780778733935 (hardcover) |
    ISBN 9780778733966 (pbk.) |
    ISBN 9781427119070 (Electronic book text)
Subjects: LCSH: Automobiles--Design and construction--Juvenile
    literature. | Automobiles--Models--Design and construction--
    Juvenile literature.
Classification: LCC TL240 .S8625 2017 (print) | LCC TL240
    (ebook) | DDC 629.222--dc23
LC record available at https://lccn.loc.gov/2016045810

Contents

SAFETY FIRST

Some of the projects in this book require scissors, sharp tools, and a hot glue gun. We recommend that children be supervised by a responsible adult for the undertaking of each project in this book.

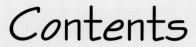

About cars

Cars as we know them today were invented in 1885. At first, cars were incredibly expensive because they were handmade. When American car manufacturer Henry Ford (left) invented the assembly line in 1913, his factory workers were able to produce cars much more quickly—and car prices tumbled. Today, there are more than a billion cars on the roads worldwide.

Car styles

Over time, the shape and color of cars have changed. These changes reflect the materials and technologies available to produce them, and the fashion of the day.

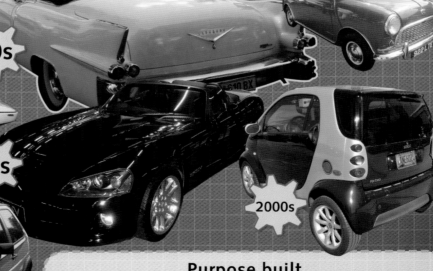

40s

60s

50s

70s

90s

2000s

80s

Purpose built

Cars are now designed to fit the needs and lifestyles of many different groups of people. **Sports utility vehicles** (SUVs), **people carriers**, **hatchbacks**, and **supercars** are just some of the different kinds of cars available.

Built for speed

Many cars are built to accelerate quickly and reach speeds much higher than the legal speed limit on the roads. For those who want to drive very fast, there are a range of motor sports available. The fastest of these is **drag racing** with a top speed of 330 mph (530 kph), followed by **Formula 1** racing, in which cars can reach a top speed of almost 230 mph (370 kph).

Built at top speed

Not only can modern cars go very fast but they are also built quickly. Using robots for much of the assembly allows manufacturers to assemble a car in approximately 67 seconds.

Cars of the future

Almost all the cars on our roads today run on gasoline or **diesel**. Burning these fuels releases gases, including carbon dioxide, which pollute the **atmosphere**. Engineers, designers, and inventors are searching for ways to design cars that use less fuel or use **dual fuel** (such as hybrid cars), electric power, **solar** power, or some other source of **energy**. Self-parking cars are a reality and designers are hard at work on **prototypes** of self-driving cars. The future of the car looks very exciting.

Before you get started on each of the projects in this book, you'll need to gather together the materials and tools listed in the "you will need" box. Hopefully you will have most things on hand, but some of the more unusual items can be bought from most hobby or electronics stores.

Balloon car

Watch this air-powered car zoom off!

How does it work? As the balloon deflates, air flows out of the drinking straw at the back of the car. The air is moving in one direction and pushes the car forward in the opposite direction. British scientist and mathematician Sir Isaac Newton explained why this happens in his Third Law of Motion: for every action there is an equal and opposite reaction.

To make a balloon car, you will need:
- corrugated cardboard, 4 inches x 7 inches (10 cm x 18 cm)
- scissors
- ruler
- paint • paintbrush
- 2 straight plastic drinking straws
- flexible plastic drinking straw
- 4 plastic bottle caps (the same size)
- 2 wooden skewers, trimmed to 5.5 inches (14 cm) long
- sticky tape
- balloon (blown up a couple of times to stretch it)

1

Paint the cardboard and leave it to dry.

2

4.7 inches (12 cm)

Use a ruler and a pair of scissors to cut each straight drinking straw to about 4.7 inches (12 cm) in length.

3

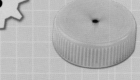

Ask an adult to poke a hole through the center of each bottle cap. The hole must be big enough for the wooden skewer to fit through.

4

0.25 inches (6 mm)

Push a wooden skewer through the hole in the bottle cap so that about a 0.25-inch (6 mm) length pokes through the hole.

5

Thread the wooden skewer through one of the drinking straws.

6

Add a second bottle cap, as you did in step 4, to create a car axle. Repeat steps 4–6 using the other skewer, remaining bottle caps, and straight drinking straw.

7

1.2 inches (3 cm)

1.2 inches (3 cm)

Tape the axles to the cardboard, 1.2 inches (3 cm) from each end.

8 Slide the end of the flexible drinking straw inside the balloon, leaving the flexible end free. Wrap sticky tape tightly around the straw and the balloon to join them together.

9

Tape the straw attached to the balloon onto the body of the car, with the flexible part of the straw bent up at one end.

10 Blow through the straw to inflate the balloon. Pinch the end of the straw to prevent air from escaping.

11 Place the balloon car on a smooth surface and let it go.

Glitch Fix!

Glitch: if the balloon will not blow up, there may be a gap in the seal between the balloon and the straw.
Fix: wind more tape tightly around the join.

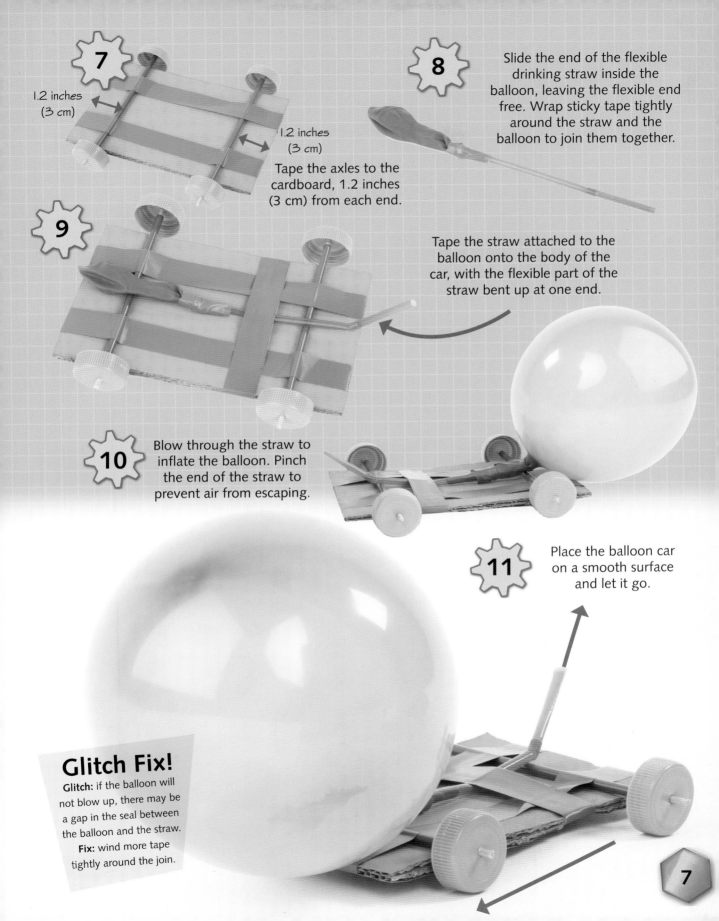

Balloon bottle car

This car is quick off the start line!

This balloon bottle car works in exactly the same way as the balloon car on pages 6–7. The car is pushed forward by the air that flows out of the drinking straw as the balloon deflates. As the air rushes out of the balloon, it creates a forward movement called **thrust**.

To make a balloon bottle car, you will need:
- small plastic juice bottle
- scissors
- 2 straight plastic drinking straws
- flexible plastic drinking straw
- 4 plastic bottle caps
- glue gun
- 2 wooden skewers, trimmed to 4.7 inches (12 cm) long
- balloon (blown up a couple of times to stretch it)
- sticky tape

1 Ask an adult to use the scissors to make a hole in the side of the plastic bottle, near the neck.

hole

2

Use scissors to trim the straight drinking straws so that they are 4 inches (10 cm) long. Follow steps 3–6 on page 6 to make two pairs of wheels and axles.

Ask an adult to supervise when you use the hot glue gun.

3 Hot glue the axles to the body of the bottle, on the opposite side to the hole you made in step 1.

4 Slide the end of the flexible drinking straw into the balloon leaving the flexible end free. Wrap sticky tape tightly around to join.

5 Slide the flexible end of the straw through the hole in the bottle and out the neck.

8

6

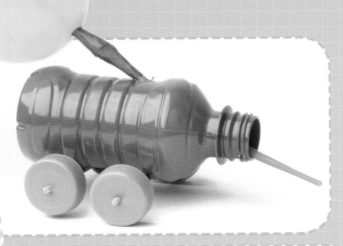

Blow through the straw to inflate the balloon. Pinch the end of the straw to prevent air from escaping. Put the balloon bottle car on a smooth surface and let it go.

A fair test

Try racing the two types of balloon cars (pages 6–9) over a measured distance to see which one goes farthest, fastest, and straightest.

To see if you can improve the performance of the winning car, make a second car that is identical except for one change (see right for suggestions). Race the cars again and record the results.

If the change you make does not improve the performance of the car, or makes it worse, change it back and think of another improvement that might work better. This way you can make your car a race winner!

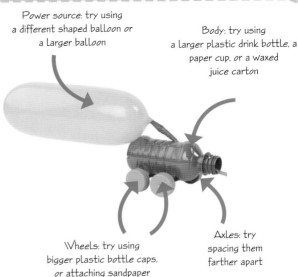

Power source: try using a different shaped balloon or a larger balloon

Body: try using a larger plastic drink bottle, a paper cup, or a waxed juice carton

Wheels: try using bigger plastic bottle caps, or attaching sandpaper strips to the wheels to improve grip

Axles: try spacing them farther apart

Is it a car or is it a rocket?

Bloodhound is a **supersonic** car that will be powered by a jet engine and a rocket. The aim is to break the current world land speed record by reaching speeds in excess of 1,000 mph (1,609 kph) and, at the same time, inspire a new generation of scientists and engineers.

Find out more about the Bloodhound Project at:

www.bloodhoundssc.com/education

Rubber band car

Is this a wind-up car?

What makes it move? By winding the chain of rubber bands around the car's axle, you have stored energy in the stretched rubber bands. When you let go of the car, the rubber bands release the energy as they return to their original shape. The energy turns the wheels and the car moves forward.

Ask an adult to supervise when you use the hot glue gun.

1 Ask an adult to poke a hole in the center of each bottle cap for the wooden dowels to fit through. Use the hot glue gun to attach a bottle cap to the center of each CD to make four wheels.

2 Cut four 0.5-inch (1.25 cm) wide pieces from the sleeve of the rubber glove. Stretch one of the pieces of rubber glove around the edge of each CD wheel. This will help the wheels grip the floor as they turn.

3 Carefully poke two holes opposite each other, about 1.5 inches (4 cm) from each end of the cardboard tube. This will form the body of the car. Push the dowels through the holes. The dowels need to be able to turn freely in the holes.

4 Push the free ends of the dowels through the center of each CD wheel. Glue them in place with the hot glue gun.

Ask an adult to supervise when you use the hot glue gun.

5

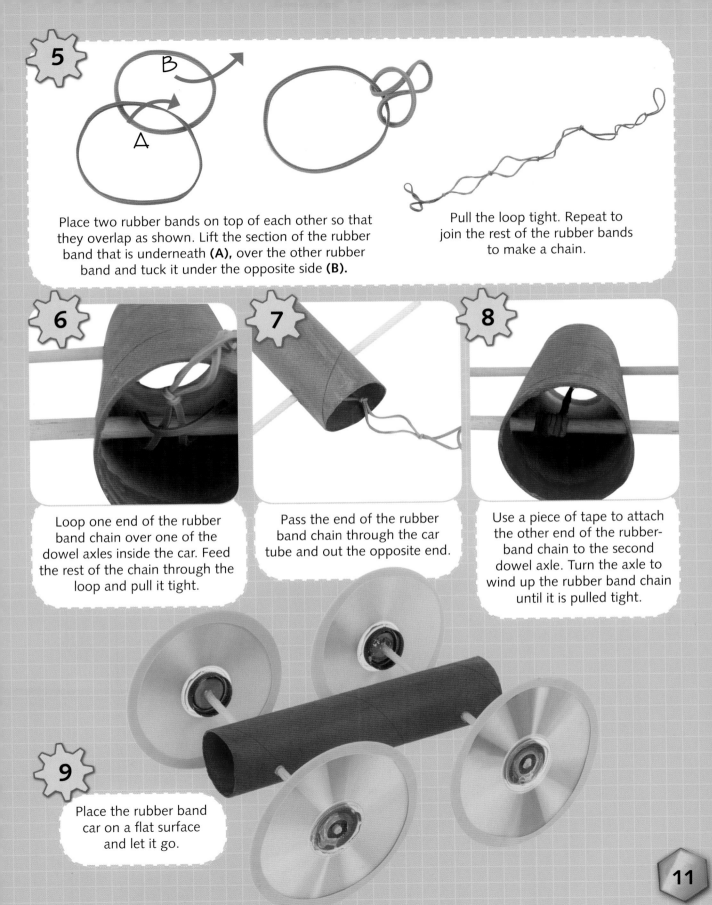

Place two rubber bands on top of each other so that they overlap as shown. Lift the section of the rubber band that is underneath **(A)**, over the other rubber band and tuck it under the opposite side **(B)**.

Pull the loop tight. Repeat to join the rest of the rubber bands to make a chain.

6

Loop one end of the rubber band chain over one of the dowel axles inside the car. Feed the rest of the chain through the loop and pull it tight.

7

Pass the end of the rubber band chain through the car tube and out the opposite end.

8

Use a piece of tape to attach the other end of the rubber-band chain to the second dowel axle. Turn the axle to wind up the rubber band chain until it is pulled tight.

9

Place the rubber band car on a flat surface and let it go.

Battery fan car

Switch on the fan to see this car whizz along the ground!

What makes it move? The fan is powered by two small batteries. When the fan is switched on, the blades spin, drawing in air and pushing it out again and away from the back of the car, which pushes the car forward.

To make a battery fan car, you will need:

- cardboard potato chip tube, including its plastic lid
- piece of wrapping paper the same length as the tube, and long enough to wrap around it with a 0.5-inch (1.25 cm) overlap
- glue stick • hot glue gun
- 4 large plastic lids (all the same size)
- 2 straight plastic drinking straws
- 2 wooden skewers
- scissors
- a small battery-operated fan

1

Wrap the wrapping paper around the cardboard tube and glue it in place with the glue stick where it overlaps.

2

Ask an adult to poke a hole in the center of each plastic lid for the wooden skewers to fit through.

3

1 inch (2.5 cm)

0.5 inches (1.25 cm)

1 inch (2.5 cm)

4

0.25 inches (6 mm)

Ask an adult to make a pair of holes about 1 inch (2.5 cm) from each end of the tube. Push a drinking straw through each pair of holes. Cut the straws so that 0.5 inches (1.25 cm) are left sticking out on either side of the tube. The straws should fit in the holes tightly. If they are loose, use the hot glue to hold them in place.

Ask an adult to supervise when you use the hot glue gun.

Push the wooden skewers through the straws. Trim the ends with scissors so that 0.25 inches (6 mm) of each skewer sticks out of each end of the straws.

12

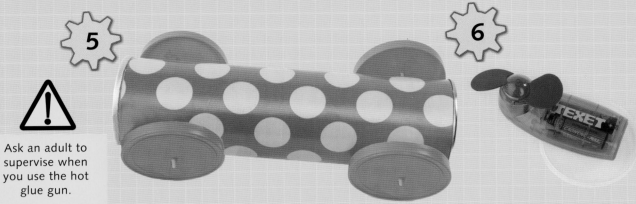

5

Ask an adult to supervise when you use the hot glue gun.

Push the wheels onto the ends of the wooden skewers. Use the hot glue gun to put a blob of glue on the end of each skewer. (The skewers need to move freely inside the drinking straws.)

6

Remove the lid from the end of the car. Use the hot glue gun to stick the battery fan to the outside of the lid so that the blades overhang.

7

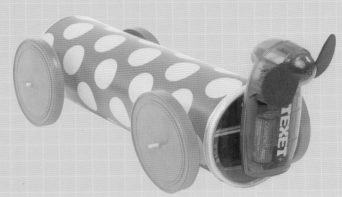

Attach the lid back onto the end of the car so that the blades of the fan are at the top.

8

Place your battery fan car on a smooth surface and switch it on.
Away it goes!

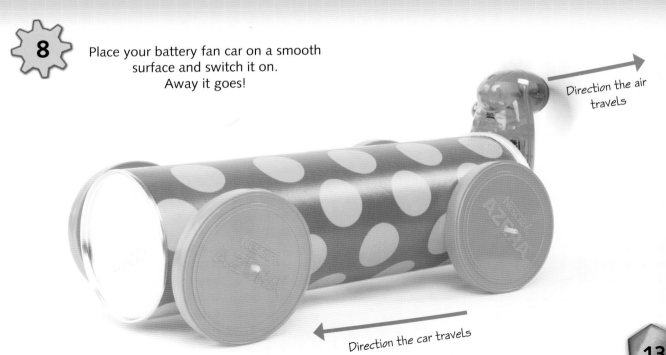

Direction the air travels

Direction the car travels

13

Propeller car

A small electric motor powers this speedy propeller car.

How does the propeller move the car? The plastic propeller is connected to a small electric motor, powered by a battery. The motor drives the propeller, which spins round and round, grabbing air and pushing it out backward, creating a thrust **force** that moves the car forward.

To make this propeller car, you will need:

- medium-sized cylindrical plastic pop or water bottle with its cap
- ruler and felt-tip pen • scissors
- 1.5–3 volt small electric motor (available from electronics or hobby stores)
- battery connector
- 4 water bottle caps (must be the same size)
- hot glue gun • 2 straight plastic drinking straws
- 2 wooden skewers
- medium-sized cuboid-shaped plastic water bottle
- battery holder and 2 AA batteries

1

Use the ruler to measure 2.4 inches (6 cm) from the top of the cylindrical bottle. Make a mark around the bottle. Cut around the top of the bottle.

2

Be careful as the plastic edge is sharp. Use scissors to make cuts 0.5 inches (13 mm) apart, cutting from the outer edge toward the bottle's neck.

3

4

Twist each of the cut pieces under and to the right to create a propeller shape.

Push the top of the bottle against a hard surface, so that the pieces fan out and bend back.

5

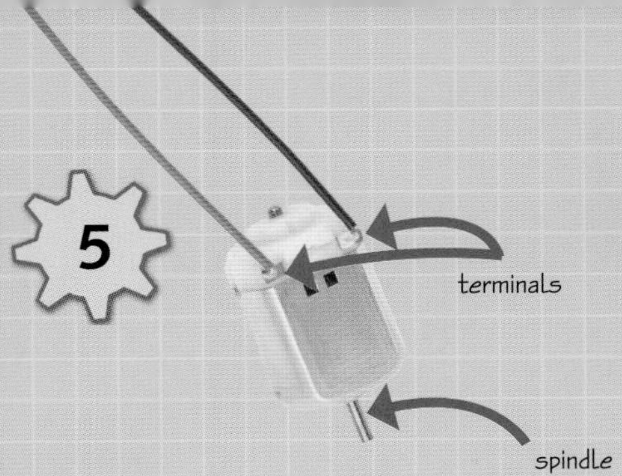

terminals

spindle

Connect the ends of the wires on the battery connector to the two terminals on the electric motor.

6 Ask an adult to poke a hole through the center of the cap from the cylindrical plastic bottle. Push the spindle of the motor through the hole.

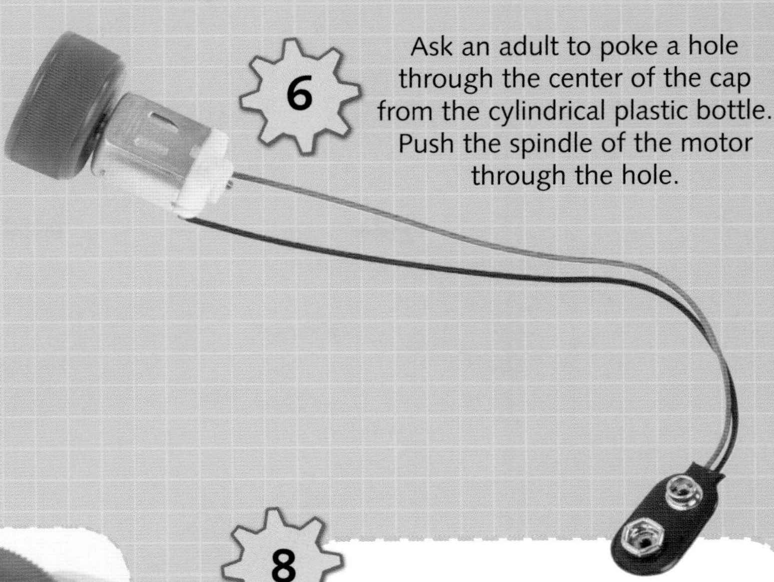

7

⚠️ Ask an adult to supervise when you use the hot glue gun.

Use a blob of hot glue to secure the spindle to the inside of the bottle top. Leave to dry.

8 Screw the propeller you made in steps 1–4 into the bottle top with the motor on it.

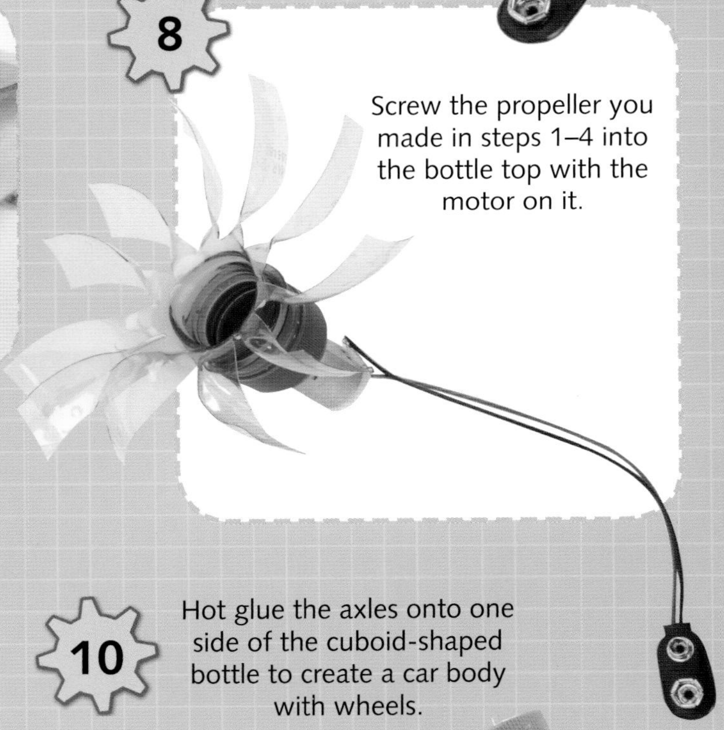

9

Follow steps 3–6 on page 6 to make wheels and axles for the car, using four bottle caps, two drinking straws, and two wooden skewers.

10 Hot glue the axles onto one side of the cuboid-shaped bottle to create a car body with wheels.

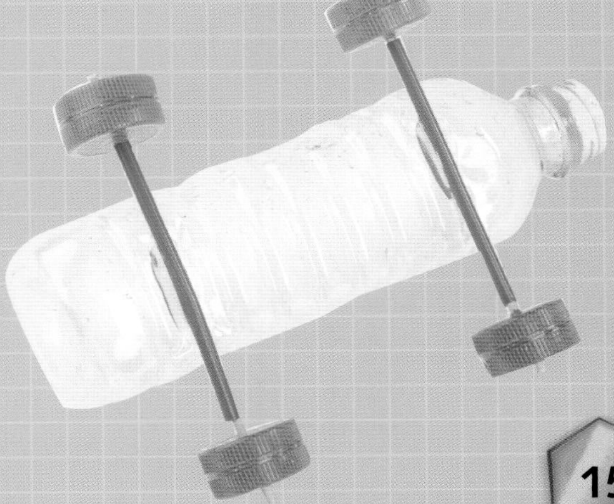

15

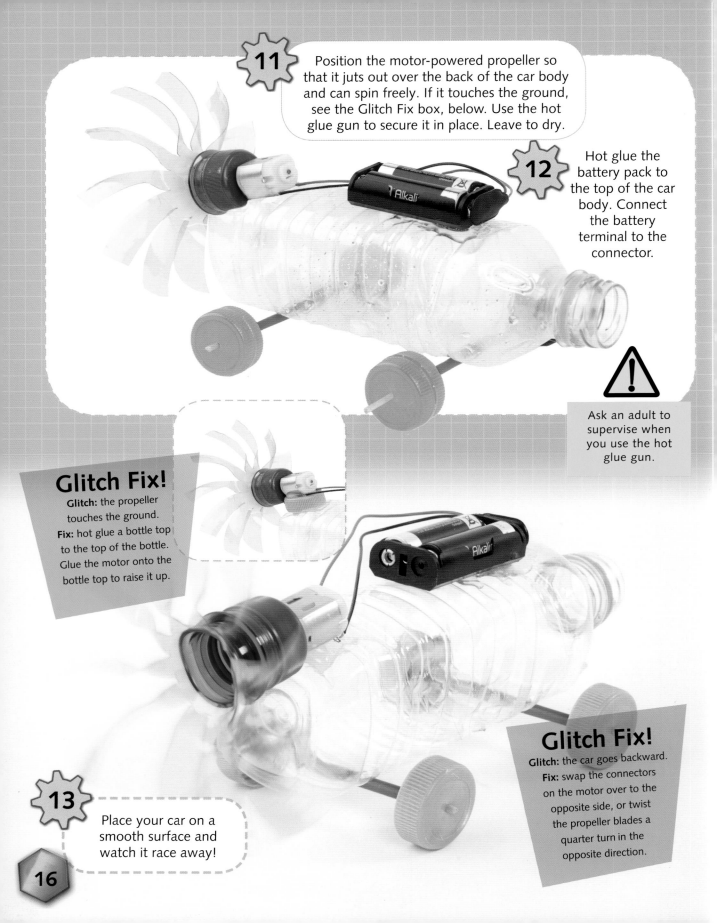

11 Position the motor-powered propeller so that it juts out over the back of the car body and can spin freely. If it touches the ground, see the Glitch Fix box, below. Use the hot glue gun to secure it in place. Leave to dry.

12 Hot glue the battery pack to the top of the car body. Connect the battery terminal to the connector.

⚠️ Ask an adult to supervise when you use the hot glue gun.

Glitch Fix!

Glitch: the propeller touches the ground.
Fix: hot glue a bottle top to the top of the bottle. Glue the motor onto the bottle top to raise it up.

Glitch Fix!

Glitch: the car goes backward.
Fix: swap the connectors on the motor over to the opposite side, or twist the propeller blades a quarter turn in the opposite direction.

13 Place your car on a smooth surface and watch it race away!

16

Car design — basics

Large teams of designers work together to produce a new car. Each team will focus on one element of the design.

Body Car designers think very carefully about the shape of a new car—its body. They want the car to move through the air as smoothly as possible, so they pay great attention to **aerodynamics**. Aerodynamics is the study of the way air moves around objects. Smooth, flat, low-to-the-ground cars move through the air much more easily than boxy, tall cars, and use less fuel as a result.

Engine The fuel that will drive the car is an important factor in designing a new car. Almost all cars today have an **internal combustion engine**. The engine works by burning a mixture of fuel and air inside a cylinder containing a piston, which is a metal rod. This creates an explosion that moves the piston down, which turns a **crankshaft** linked to the wheels.

To watch a video showing how a car engine works, go to: www.sciencekids.co.nz/videos/engineering/carengine.html

Gears Gears allow the wheels to move at variable speeds. A low gear allows the wheels to turn slowly but with a strong force. So a low gear is good for climbing hills or getting the car moving from a standstill. If the car is moving on a flat surface and does not need much power, then a higher gear allows the engine to put more of its power into making speed.

When these gears turn, the smaller one will go faster and turn more times than the larger one.

To watch a video showing how gears work, go to: www.sciencekids.co.nz/videos/physics/gears.html

Car design — safety and comfort

As well as designing cars that look great and drive well, car designers and engineers build in some or all of the features below. These will ensure that their cars are safe and comfortable to drive.

Crumple zones
Areas at the front, back and sides of a car are designed to crumple to absorb the impact in a collision and offer protection to the occupants.

Airbags
Up to four airbags at the front and sides inflate to help reduce the impact on occupants during a collision.

Side impact bars
Strengthened bars along the side of the car help reduce the effects of a side impact on occupants involved in a collision.

Air conditioning
Clean air of the correct temperature is important to keep the occupants comfortable and the driver alert.

ABS brakes
An anti-lock braking system (ABS) prevents skidding and allows the driver to retain control in the event of a skid.

Seat belts
In many countries, wearing a seat belt in a car is required by law. Seat belts keep the wearer in their seat and stop them from hitting the windshield or the seat in front in a collision. Wearing a seatbelt can reduce your chance of dying in the event of a car crash by 50 percent.

Collapsible steering column
The column that the steering wheel is attached to is designed to collapse if there is an accident. This is to prevent it from hurting drivers if they are thrown forward.

Car interior People may spend many hours in their car, so it is vital that they are comfortable. Car seats are designed to give support and comfort to the occupants, and dashboard controls are placed within reach of the driver to prevent accidents. The science behind these decisions is called **ergonomics**. Car seats, steering wheels, and headrests are all adjustable to suit people of all heights and sizes.

Bottle racer

Use light materials to make this speedy model racing car!

How does it move? The bottle racer's small electric motor drives a spindle, which is connected to one of the bottle racer's wheel axles. As the spindle spins, it drives the wheels round and moves the car forward.

To make a bottle racer, you will need:
- plastic bottle with a squirt-top cap
- 4 squirt-top caps from plastic bottles, one with the lid
- 2 wooden skewers, trimmed to 4 inches (10 cm) long
- 2 straight plastic drinking straws, trimmed to 3 inches (8 cm) long
- hot glue gun
- scissors
- empty, or partly empty, ballpoint pen refill
- 1.5–3 v small electric motor (available from electronics or hobby stores)
- battery connector
- battery pack
- scraps of foam board
- sticky tape
- small rubber band

1 Ask an adult to cut out the central section of the bottle.

2

⚠️ Ask an adult to supervise when you use the hot glue gun.

Put a blob of hot glue inside one of the plastic bottle caps. Push the end of a wooden skewer into the glue. Hold it upright until the glue begins to set and leave it to set until hard. Repeat with a second bottle cap and skewer.

3  Fill these bottle caps with more glue from the hot glue gun. Leave to harden.

4 Slide the skewers with the bottle caps attached inside the drinking straws to make axles for your car.

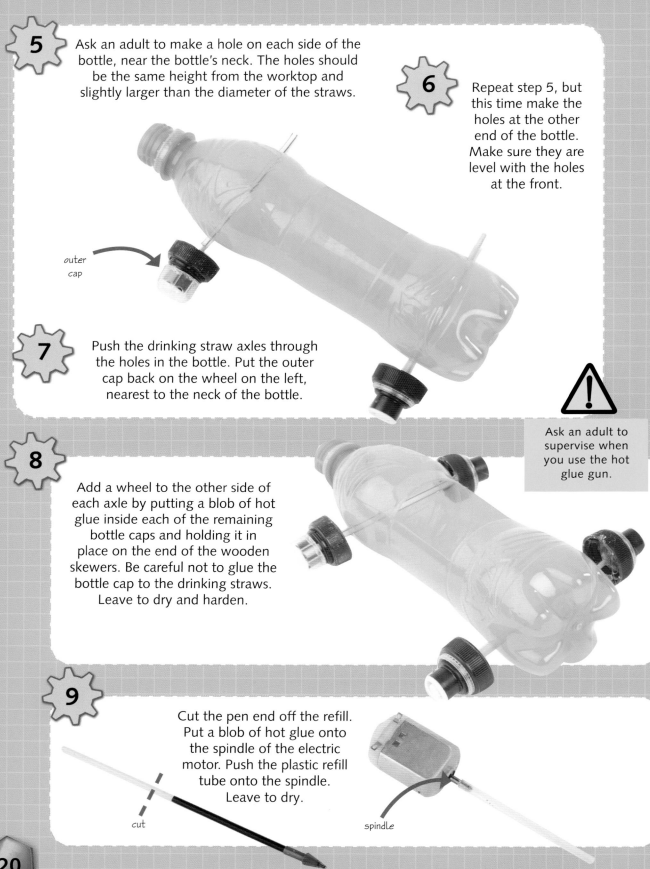

5 Ask an adult to make a hole on each side of the bottle, near the bottle's neck. The holes should be the same height from the worktop and slightly larger than the diameter of the straws.

6 Repeat step 5, but this time make the holes at the other end of the bottle. Make sure they are level with the holes at the front.

outer cap

7 Push the drinking straw axles through the holes in the bottle. Put the outer cap back on the wheel on the left, nearest to the neck of the bottle.

Ask an adult to supervise when you use the hot glue gun.

8 Add a wheel to the other side of each axle by putting a blob of hot glue inside each of the remaining bottle caps and holding it in place on the end of the wooden skewers. Be careful not to glue the bottle cap to the drinking straws. Leave to dry and harden.

9 Cut the pen end off the refill. Put a blob of hot glue onto the spindle of the electric motor. Push the plastic refill tube onto the spindle. Leave to dry.

cut

spindle

10

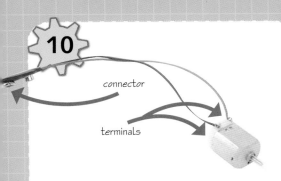

connector

terminals

Connect the ends of the wires on the battery connector to the two terminals on the electric motor.

11

hole

Ask an adult to make a hole in the side of the bottle. It should be level with the top of the front left wheel.

12

Turn the car around. Working from inside the body of the bottle racer, slide the motor's spindle tube through the hole you created in step 11. Cut some small pieces of foam board and place them under the motor until the spindle is level. Use the hot glue gun to fix the foam board in place and glue the motor on top.

foam board

13

Ask an adult to supervise when you use the hot glue gun.

Hot glue the bottom of the battery pack alongside the motor. Make sure that it does not touch the wheel axle. Leave enough space to connect the battery to the motor using the connector.

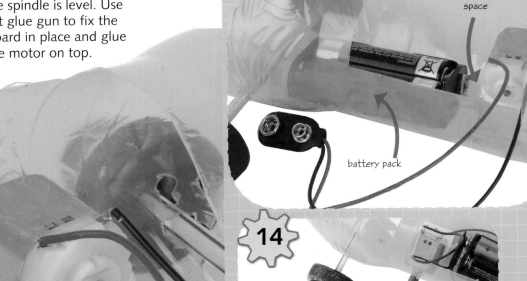

space

battery pack

14

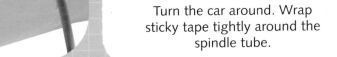

Turn the car around. Wrap sticky tape tightly around the spindle tube.

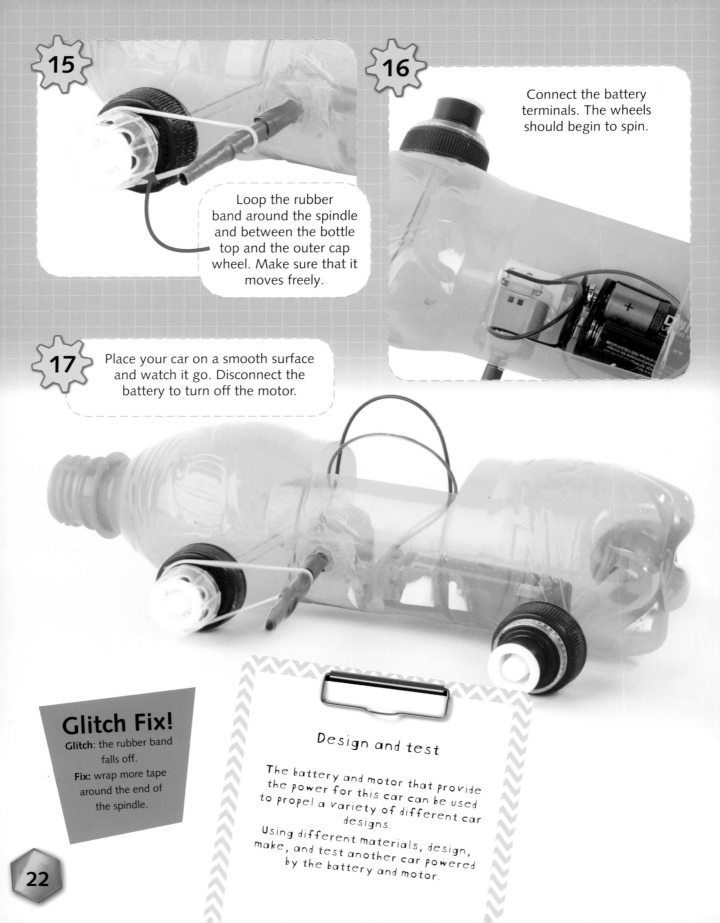

15

Loop the rubber band around the spindle and between the bottle top and the outer cap wheel. Make sure that it moves freely.

16

Connect the battery terminals. The wheels should begin to spin.

17

Place your car on a smooth surface and watch it go. Disconnect the battery to turn off the motor.

Glitch Fix!

Glitch: the rubber band falls off.
Fix: wrap more tape around the end of the spindle.

Design and test

The battery and motor that provide the power for this car can be used to propel a variety of different car designs.

Using different materials, design, make, and test another car powered by the battery and motor.

Car with gears

See how gear wheels transfer energy in this model car.

What's going on here? The gear box kit includes an electric motor powered by batteries. The spindle on the motor is attached to a gear wheel attached to a metal axle, which becomes the back axle of this car. When you turn the motor on, it turns the back axle of the car, making it move forward.

To make this car with gears, you will need:

- pencil and thin white paper (for tracing the template)
- scissors • foam board
- black acrylic paint
- orange acrylic paint
- paintbrush • silver duct tape
- ruler • hot glue gun
- straight plastic drinking straw
- 4 plastic lids from potato chip cans (must all be same size)
- wooden skewer, trimmed to 5 inches (13 cm) long
- 3 v worm drive gear box kit, including battery holder (available from electronics or hobby stores)
- 2 AA batteries
- 2 thin pieces of card stock, 0.5 inches x 3 inches (1.25 cm x 7.6 cm)

1 With thin white paper, trace and cut out the template on page 29. Use that template to cut two car shapes from the foam board. Paint one side of each foam car shape black. Leave to dry. Paint and design the other side of each car shape with the orange paint. Leave to dry.

2 Use the paper template again to cut two window shapes out of silver duct tape. Attach the windows to the foam board car shapes.

3 Use the paper template to make two marks on each of the foam board cars. Use the point of the scissors to make a small hole at each mark.

Ask an adult to supervise when you use the hot glue gun.

4

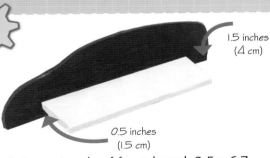

1.5 inches (4 cm)

0.5 inches (1.5 cm)

Cut a rectangle of foam board, 2.5 x 6.7 inches (6.5 x 17 cm). With the hot glue gun, glue along one long edge and attach it to the black side of one of the car shapes, 0.5 inches (1.5 cm) from the bottom edge and 1.5 inches (4 cm) from the back edge.

5

Ask an adult to make a hole in the center of each plastic lid for the wooden skewers to fit through.

6

Push the wooden skewer through the hole in one of the plastic lids so that the end pokes through slightly. Hot glue the end in place.

7

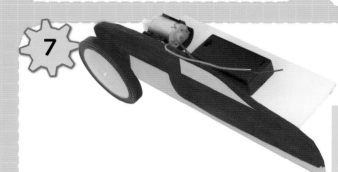

Using the above photo as reference, take the worm drive gear box with the metal axle attached to it and push the axle through the hole in the foam board car. Slide on one of the lid wheels. Glue the bottom of the gear box casing to the rectangular foam board, positioning it at the back of the car. Glue the bottom of the battery holder to the central section of the foam board.

8

Ask an adult to supervise when you use the hot glue gun.

Spread glue on the free edge of the rectangular foam board. Guide the other end of the metal axle through the small hole in the second foam board car, and hold the foam board pieces together until they set. Leave to dry.

9

Push the drinking straw through the remaining holes at the front of the foam board car shapes. Slide the wooden skewer with a wheel attached into the straw. Add another wheel to the free end of the skewer. Hot glue in place.

Slide the remaining wheel onto the metal back axle. Put a blob of hot glue in the center of each wheel to secure them all in place.

10

Cut a rectangle of foam board 3 inches x 1 inch (8 cm x 2.5 cm). Paint it and leave to dry.

Cover the two pieces of thin card stock with silver duct tape.

Ask an adult to supervise when you use the hot glue gun.

Hot glue the pieces of silver card stock on either side of the foam board, to create a **spoiler**.

Glue the spoiler onto the outside of the back of the car at a 45 degree angle.

11 Connect the metal ends of the red and black wires to the two battery terminals. Bend the metal wires back to keep them in place.

12 Place the car on a smooth surface. Switch it on and watch the gear wheel turn the back axle.

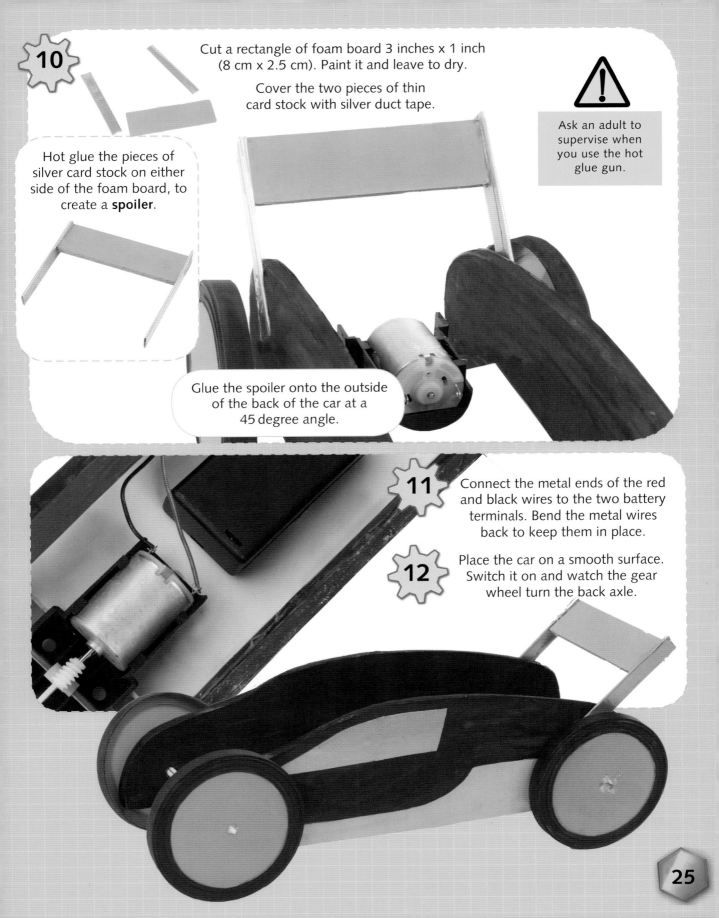

Solar car

This eco car is powered by the Sun.

How does it work? The solar panel on the top of the car is coated in a special material that absorbs sunlight and converts it into electrical energy. This energy travels down the wires to drive the motor, which is attached to a propeller. The propeller whizzes around, sucking in air and pushing it out backward, which moves the car forward.

To make this solar car, you will need:

- pencil and thin white paper (for tracing the template)
- scissors • ruler
- foam board
- hot glue gun • paint and paintbrush • metal skewer
- 2 straight plastic drinking straws
- 2 wooden skewers
- micro motor (4 v solar micro motor 47,000 rpm) propeller, and solar panel kit (available from electronics and hobby stores)
- small screwdriver
- 2 polystyrene balls, 1.5 inches (4 cm) in diameter
- 2 polystyrene balls, 0.5 inches (1.5 cm) in diameter

1

Use the paper and pencil to trace the template on page 29. Cut it out and use it to cut out four triangular shapes from the foam board.

2

Glue the four foam triangles together, matching up the edges. Paint and leave to dry.

3

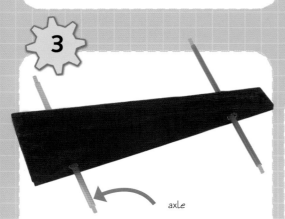

axle

Use the metal skewer to make two holes through the foam board triangles. Use the paper template from step 1 to help you choose the right place. Push the drinking straws through the holes and slide the wooden skewers through the straws to create two axles.

4

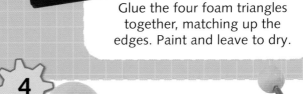

Place the foam car body on the work surface. Push a larger polystyrene ball onto each end of the back axle. Make sure that the foam ball does not touch the drinking straw.

Push a smaller polystyrene ball onto each end of the front axle. Make sure that all the wheels turn freely on the axles.

5 Use the screwdriver to slightly loosen the screws in the plastic connection box, leaving a small space under the tip of each screw.

Slide the metal end of the red wire from the solar panel under the tip of the screw marked A. Tighten the screw to hold it in place.

Slide the metal end of the red wire from the propeller under the tip of the screw marked C. Tighten the screw to hold it in place.

Slide the metal end of the black wire from the solar panel under the tip of the screw marked B. Tighten the screw to hold it in place.

Slide the metal end of the black wire from the propeller under the tip of the screw marked D. Tighten the screw to hold it in place.

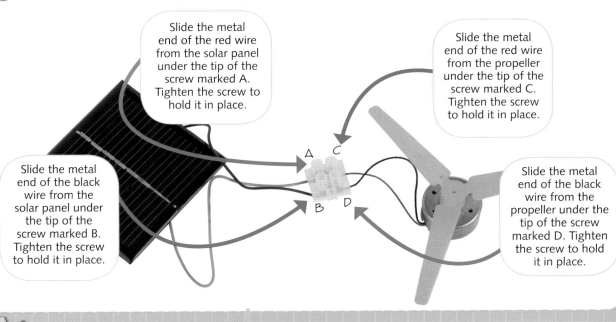

6

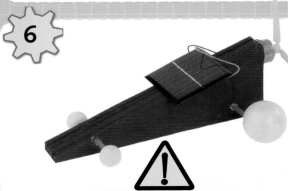

Use the hot glue gun to attach the back of the solar panel to the top of the foam car body.

⚠️ Ask an adult to supervise when you use the hot glue gun.

7 Hot glue the base of the micro motor propeller onto the back of the foam car body. The propeller must be positioned high enough so that it has room to turn.

8

Leave the completed car for a few minutes where strong sunlight will fall on the solar panel. If there is no strong sunlight, shine a bright lamp onto it instead. Place the car on the ground and switch it on to watch it go!

Milestones in the history of cars

1769

Frenchman Nicolas-Joseph Cugnot designed a steam-powered tricycle, capable of carrying four people. This was the world's first mechanical vehicle.

1826

Samuel Brown of England invented a gas engine to propel a road vehicle. He has been called "the father of the gas engine."

1859/60

Frenchman Gaston Planté invented rechargeable batteries. This led to the development of **electric cars**.
In Belgium, Etienne Lenoir patented the first two-stroke gas engine.

1876

German Nikolaus Otto invented the four-stroke internal combustion engine.

1885/6

In Germany, Karl Benz built a two-seater tricycle powered by a four-stroke gas engine and patented it the following year. In 1886, Gottlieb Daimler and Wilhelm Maybach built a four-wheel, four-stroke gas-engine car.

1903

American Henry Ford formed the Ford Motor Company in Detroit, Michigan.

1904

Henry Ford created Ford of Canada in Walkerville, Ontario.

1906

A Stanley steam car achieved 120 mph (193 kph) to break the land speed record. Steam-powered cars shared the roads with both gas and electric cars at this time.

1907

Canada's first gas station opened in Vancouver, British Columbia.

1908

The Ford Motor Company began producing the Model T car.

1911

American Charles Kettering invented the first electric car starter.

1913

Henry Ford introduced the assembly line into his car factory in Detroit, Michigan.

1924

The building of the world's first highway was completed in Italy.

1934

A major shift in car design began with the rounded features of the Chrysler Airflow.

1951

John W. Hetrick invented the airbag in Newport, Pennsylvania.

1971

Canadian Parliament passed the Motor Vehicle Safety Act, outlining new standards for the design and construction of motor vehicles.

1990s

The scientific community agreed that car emissions were contributing to **climate change.** This has led to the research and manufacture of greener, more **fuel-efficient** cars.

2010

The number of cars on the road worldwide reached one billion.

Today

Hybrid cars and electric cars exist alongside conventional gas-fueled cars. A prototype of a driverless car has been made.

Templates

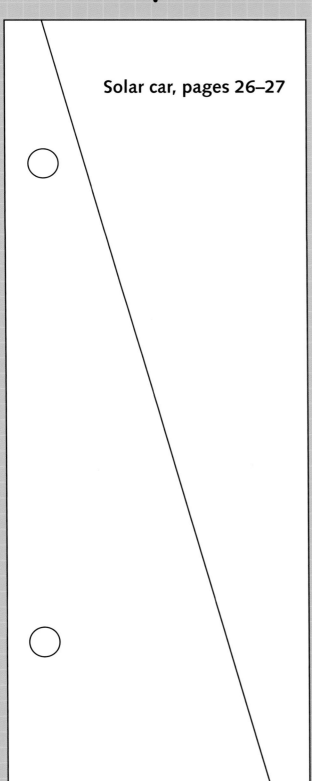

Solar car, pages 26–27

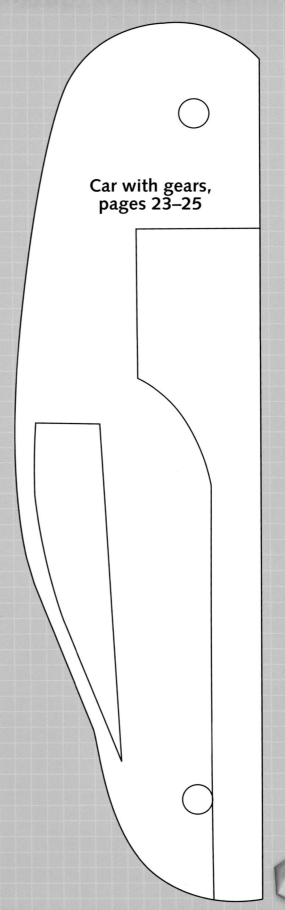

Car with gears,
pages 23–25

29

Glossary

aerodynamics The study of air and how objects move through it

assembly line A line of workers and machines performing a particular task as they assemble a product, which is moving in front of them inside a factory

atmosphere The layer of protective gases that surrounds planet Earth

climate change Changes in the world's weather that most people believe are a result of human activity on Earth

crankshaft A long metal rod that helps the engine turn the wheels

diesel A liquid fuel derived from oil

drag racing A type of motor sport in which two vehicles compete side-by-side to be the fastest to cover a short distance from a standing start

dual fuel Capable of running on two fuels; One fuel is usually gasoline or diesel and the other is a less polluting fuel, such as natural gas or hydrogen

eco Not harming the environment

electric car A car powered by rechargeable batteries

energy The ability to do work. It comes in several forms, including heat, light, chemical energy, and electricity

ergonomics The science of how to better design and arrange things so that people can work more safely and efficiently

force A push or a pull

Formula 1 The most popular form of world motor racing

fuel efficient The way an engine works, to waste as little fuel as possible

gear One of a set of toothed wheels that work together to alter the relationship between the (car) engine and the speed of the driven parts (the wheels)

hatchback A car with a door at the back that opens upward, giving full access to the truck or back for loading

internal combustion engine An engine that generates moving power by mixing fuel and air inside the engine to create an explosion that moves a piston or pistons, joined to other moving parts

people carrier A car with three rows of seats, allowing the vehicle to carry more passengers than a normal car

propeller A revolving shaft with two or more angled blades attached to it, used for propelling a boat or aircraft

prototype A first or early version of a design or vehicle, from which others will be developed

solar Relating to the Sun; Solar power is the conversion of sunlight into electrical energy

spoiler A device that functions to increase a car's grip on the road

sports utility vehicle (SUV) A four-wheel-drive car capable of driving in on-road and off-road driving conditions

supercar A high-performance sports car

supersonic To move at up to five times the speed of sound

thrust A pushing force that moves something forward

Learning More

Books

Graham, Ian. *Cars: Design and Engineering for STEM*. Heinemann-Raintree, 2013.

Mattern, Joanne. *A Visit to a Car Factory*. Teacher Created Materials, 2011.

Morganelli, Adrianna. *Formula One*. Crabtree Publishing, 2007.

Websites

Learn all about the Bloodhound model rocket car challenge here:

**www.bloodhoundssc.com/news/bloodhound-model-rocket
-car-challenge**

Use this link to find out how your school can take part in a world record attempt for the fastest rocket-powered model car:

**www.guinnessworldrecords.com/news/2015/8/video-bloodhound-
project-how-you-can-take-part-in-a-world-record-attempt-for-391281**

Learn how to construct a car at this site:

**www.mylearning.org/intermediate-interactive.
asp?type=4&journeyid=337**

Check out this amazing site for animations and information about how a car is made:

www.toyota.co.jp/en/kids/car/test.html

Index